Between Black Women

Listening With the Third Ear

by

Joy Jones

Chicago, Illinois

Illustration by Reginald Mackey

Back cover photo by Stephen A. Parham

First edition, first printing

Copyright ©1994 by Joy Jones

Printed in the United States of America

ISBN 0-913543-40-3

Between Black Women
Listening With the Third Ear

by

Joy Jones

Dedication

To my mother, Marilyn F. Jones, who gave me the discipline to say no; and to my father, W. Morgan Jones, who showed me the joy of saying yes.

Acknowledgments

Grateful thanks to the listening ears of:

The Creator; my current and former co-workers in the Office of Gender Equity - Larice Boseman, Eleanor Elie, Richard Graydon, Rhoda Green, Lamar McClain, Stephen Parham, and S. Michele Rucker; and my colleagues from the EEO Office of the D.C. Public Schools - Emanuel Carr, Jeanette Johnson, Joyce King, Barbara Lucas, and Marie Mitchell.

Special thanks to Eddie Colbert, Carroll Gibbs, Jackie Grice, Eunice Wright Jones, Stephen Monroe, Ann Shelton, Beverly Townes, Ronald Wildy, Tyrone Woods, Harvest R. Williams, Jr., and Darnell Yelder.

Chapter 3 originally appeared in modified version in *The Washington Post*, Outlook section, September 1, 1991.

Table of Contents

Dedication
Acknowledgments

Chapter 1
Those Who Listen, Gain All 1

Chapter 2
The Power of Listening 5

Chapter 3
Do You Know this Woman? 11

Chapter 4
The Change Within 19

Chapter 5
Feminine Energy, Feminine Strength 29

Chapter 6
The Single Life 45

Chapter 7
Positive Images, Positive Relationships 61

Chapter 8
Cooperation in the Face of a Crisis 73

References 91

Notes

1

Those Who Listen, Gain All

If it had not been for storytelling, the Black family would not have survived.

-Jackie Torrence

Two women sat together making calabashes - one old, one young. The old woman set her calabash in the dirt beside her and turned to her young friend. "Young woman," she said, "what is better - to have gold, children or the power of listening?"

"Old woman, I need cash and desire children; two ears I already have, but I know you and how you think: You would say it is the power of listening that is best."

"So you say, then young one, I must tell you a story to prove it to you. Put on your third ear!" This is the tale she told.

Near the banks of a tropical river, a long time ago, there lived a husband and wife. To clothe themselves, they wore whatever discarded rags they could find. They ate whatever remained clinging to stalks after the pickers had collected their harvest. They had no children. The wife

1

prayed for better days, but nothing ever seemed to yield. So, they made peace with their meager possessions.

This couple had one friend, a man by the name of Abinuku, which means "angry-with-the-world." He would visit the poor couple from time to time, offering them complaints from his bitter heart, though he considered himself a friend. He happened to be at the couple's home at the time Providence fulfilled the wife's prayers.

Three blessings were sent to the husband and wife. The blessings were Gold, a Child and Power of Listening. As the three blessings made their way to the couple's dwelling, they came to a river. "I am precious," said Gold to Child, "carry me across in your arms."

"No, I'm too young," cried Child to Gold. "You should support me on your back." They argued at length while Power of Listening waited patiently. They exhausted themselves in anger, until finally Power of Listening took each by the hand and guided them through the stream.

After several suns and several moons and many footsteps through the forest, the three blessings arrived at the home of the couple. "Oh, look how we have been blessed!" cried the wife to her husband, as she gave thanks through prayer. But during her prayer, the Divine revealed to her that she could only choose one blessing. Gold, the Child and Power of Listening would be visitors for only seven days, after which the couple would have to pick the one guest they wanted to stay.

"Ah, what a hard decision," said the husband to his wife. "Perhaps we should ask someone's advice."

"Maybe I can help," said Abinuku, quick to jump in. (He was resentful of the couple's good fortune.) "Money comes and quickly goes. Children grow up and eventually leave home; so you should choose the power of listening

because it will always be with you," advised Abinuku, thinking he had recommended the least valuable choice. They took his advice and kept Power of Listening, sadly sending the other two blessings on their way.

Gold and the Child headed back. Along the way, they encountered the same river where they had met. Once again they argued about how to cross it. They fought from dusk until dawn, but still they could not come to any agreement. Since they could not get back to their home, they decided to turn around and make the poor couple's house their new home.

When Gold and the Child returned to the poor couple's house, they were received with much rejoicing. They all feasted, danced and celebrated throughout the entire village. Abinuku, of course, walked off in disgust.

"You see," said the old woman to the young woman as she picked up her calabash, "blessings are given to the one who chooses to listen. Good gifts abound for those who honor the power of listening. Those who are able to listen and show patience will gain all."

"But do not misunderstand my meaning, for if a lion is attacking you, that is not the time to wait and listen. That is the time to run."

2

The Power of Listening

Music and speech are considered potent forces ... because they are phenomena of the invisible world. We cannot see them, yet their impact on us can be profound.

-Yaya Diallo

Ours is an oral tradition. From the revered riots of West Africa to the rappers on the latest music videos, people of African descent, like most cultures, delight and excel in telling stories. Our tradition includes Anansi and Brer Rabbit, Stagolee and Shango, Mahalia singing spirituals and Smoky crooning love ballads. Insight and revelation are the gifts of the story that enhance the entertainment.

But ours is also an aural tradition - one of listening to the words and the music, to what is spoken and to what is left unsaid then responding to each accordingly. As much as we value the spoken word, much of human communication takes place in the realm of the non-verbal. What's hidden behind the words? What's in the spaces between the lines? What is the moral of the story? These are the places where the messages lie.

Although stories tell the history of a people, they are not always totally accurate. Oral histories convey not just the factual account of what happened, but the spirit, culture and meaning of what happened. The listener understands in the subtleties of a turn of phrase, the cadence of speech, the tone of voice.

Listening to a spoken story or music engages the listener to be both quiet and responsive. Quiet, so the story can be heard. Responsive because the drama of the words and rhythms compels reaction. A good story will trigger feelings, stimulate reflection, then lead to action.

Listening is a discipline. Often regarded as a passive act, listening is quite an active task. To listen, one must be fully present. The listener must be involved. If one does not immerse oneself in the story, he or she will miss the most important parts - those things which are not conveyed directly - the implicit, the hidden, the deep.

Listening teaches skills in managing paradox. The listener is still, yet active. The listener is present in the "hear" and now, although immersed in a world created of another time and place. Listeners pay attention to the words, but absorb much of the meaning from the hidden messages between each word. Listening to a story or song grips the listener even as he or she surrenders to it. But this surrender is not one of loss. It is the type of surrender where one relinquishes one thing in order to receive something else of greater value.

Listening is good practice for learning to embrace life. After all, life itself is a matter of call and response - how we respond to God's call in building relationships with each other. It is a straightforward call, but it must be fulfilled in the context of the paradoxes of everyday life. Many adults have even discovered that many of the great spiritual truths are paradoxes: "The more you know, the more you don't know," or "In yielding, there is strength."

There must be some technique for living in this paradox. I imagine that the right balance is similar to great jazz. Multiple rhythms and diverse chords playing simultaneously produce discord in the hands of the inexperienced. However, in the hands of one who develops a feel and an ear for the music, the result is harmony. Finding the balance point is not always easy, but it beats living at either extreme of the scale. Thus, explains the power of listening.

Frequently, when people talk about what a relationship needs to succeed, the first word mentioned is *communication*. It's the universal mantra of marriage counselors, pop psych gurus and frustrated lovers everywhere. When we think of communication, we generally think of passionately expressing whatever it is we have burning on our lips to be spoken. But communication is a dance with two partners, a speaker and a listener. The latter might even be the more telling half - absorbing all that is said and discerning that which is too difficult to be said or is too complex to be reduced to mere words is often the part that makes the critical difference. Listening is a call and response of a higher order.

Have you ever tried to tell somebody how moving you found a particular song? You recite the words to the tune, but somehow the lyrics sound flat and silly when divorced from the music. Together, however, the passion of the singer wedded to the emotion of the music evokes a meaning that is deeper, wiser and more profound than any one of them alone. You cannot explain it, you can only hear it and know.

Finding that mid-point - that centered place - requires listening with the third ear. That ear, based at the core of the word heart. I find it significant that the very word *heart* literally has *ear* at it's center. There is a section of West Africa where storytellers begin each story saying, "How many ears do you have?" The audience calls back "Two!" The storyteller then says, "Well, put on your third ear to hear this story!" Listening with the third ear allows you to hear and understand the whole story, interpret the whole song.

It is the third ear that discerns truth, not just in facts, figures, hard news and headlines, but also in poetry, literature, stories and songs. The third ear knows that wisdom for living is not learned only in college classrooms or from Sunday school lessons, but is picked up in conversations overheard as a child who the grown-ups thought was asleep. These are ancient stories handed down over generations; heart-to-hearts with your best girlfriend, your mother, your man; or from the wail of a blues woman, or the shout of sister singing spirituals.

As you read the following chapters, you will find lessons from the ancient tradition of storytelling as well as anecdotes from the lives of everyday people. Insights about men, femininity, and relationships have come about in the unexpected context of singing, dancing and storytelling. These arts became vehicles by which I learned to live the paradox that is life. Responding to music and dance provides a model for learning how to embrace flexible thinking and the rhythm of give and take in relationships. It is not by happenstance that our forebearers marked major transitions of life with rituals of story, dance and music. These primal elements invite the participant to both lose herself and find herself, to surrender in order to transcend, to become strong by becoming vulnerable, to understand the woman that she is and is becoming - all achieved by listening with the third ear.

3

Do You Know This Woman?

I will look at me before I look for love.

- Iyanla Vanzant

Have you met this woman? She has a good job, works hard, and earns a good salary. She went to college, even got her master's degree; she is a very intelligent woman. She works hard at her job, and is rewarded for it. She is personable, articulate, well-read, interested in everybody and everything. Yet, she's single.

Or, maybe you know this sister. She's active in the church. Faithful and committed, she loves the Lord and knows God's Word. You'd think that with her command of the scriptures and the respect of her church members, she'd have a marriage as solid as a rock. But again, there is no husband.

Perhaps you might even recognize the community activist sister. She's a Black woman on the move - or as she prefers to acknowledge herself - an African American woman. She sports a short natural, maybe cornrow braids or even dreadlocks. She's an organizer, a motivator, a dynamo. Her work for her people speaks for itself - organizing women for a self-help collective, raising funds for a community cause, educating others around still another issue in South Africa. Black folks look up to her, and white folks know she's a force to be reckoned with. Yet once again, the men folk find that a relationship with her is difficult, at best.

What do these women have in common? Seemingly, they all have it together, so what is it that they lack? Why is it they may be able to hook a man but cannot hold onto him?

These women puzzle over this dilemma themselves. They gather together at their professional clubs, sorority meetings or over coffee at the office and wonder what's wrong with Black men. They hold special prayer vigils, fasting and praying and begging Jesus to send them [the brothers] back to church. They find the brothers attending the strategizing session or participating in the protest, but when it comes time to go home, the brothers go home to someone else.

I know these women because I am these women. After asking over and over again, "What's wrong with these men?' it finally dawned on me to ask the question, "What's wrong with us women?"

What I have found, and what many of these women have yet to discover, is that the skills that make one successful in the church, community or workplace are *not* the skills that make one successful in a relationship.

Linear thinking, self-reliance, structured goals and direct action assist one in getting assignments done, in organizing church or club members for an activity or in positioning oneself for a raise. But relationship-building requires different skills. It requires making decisions that not only gratify you, but satisfy others. It means doing those things that will keep the peace rather than achieve the goal. Sometimes it means you first have to create the peace before it can be kept. Maintaining a harmonious relationship will not always allow you to take the straight line approach when you need to travel the distance between two points. You may have to stoop to conquer or yield to win. In all too many cases when dealing with men, you will have to sacrifice the satisfaction of being right in order to enjoy the satisfaction of being loved. Being acknowledged as the head of the household is especially important to men, since their manhood is so often actively challenged everywhere else.

Many modern women are so independent, so self-sufficient, so committed to the cause, to Christ, to career - or their narrow concept of one - that their whole personalities project an "I don't need a man" attitude. They end up without one although that is seldom their intent. An interested man may be attracted but he soon discovers that this sister makes very little space for him in her life.

Going to graduate school is a good goal and an option that previous generations of Blacks have not had. But sometimes the achieving woman will place her boyfriend so low on her list of things to do that his interest wanes. Between work, school and homework, she's seldom *there* for him, to do the things a man views as preliminary before he develops a commitment to a woman. She's too busy to prepare him a home-cooked meal or to be a listening ear for his concerns because she is so occupied by her own. Soon he uses her for uncommitted sex since - to him - she is unavailable for anything else. Blind to the part she's playing in the problem, she ends up thinking, "Men only want one thing," then she decides that she's better off with the degree than the friendship. When she's 45, she may wish she'd set different priorities while she was younger. It's true - it is hard to go into graduate school at age 45, but it's even harder to find a husband.

It's not just the busy career woman who cannot see the forest for the trees. A couple I know was having marital troubles. During one argument, the husband confronted the wife and asked what she thought they should do about the marriage, what direction did she think they should take. She reached for her Bible and turned to Ephesians. "I know what Paul says and I know what Jesus says about marriage," he told her, "What do YOU say about our marriage?" Like so many of us, she could recite the scriptures, but she could not personalize them into everyday living. Before the year was out, the husband had filed for divorce.

Women who focus on civil rights or community activism have vigorous, fighting spirits and are prepared to do whatever, whenever to benefit African American people. That's good. It needs to be done. But it needs to be kept in perspective. It's too easy to save the world and lose your man - and not because of the White man or other women, Black or White. A fighting spirit is good on the battlefield, but it's a gentler spirit that's wanted on the homefront. Too many of these women are winning the battle and losing the home.

Sometimes in the very sincere and determined effort to be a strong believer or a hard worker, we contemporary women down-play, denigrate - or simply forget - our more traditional feminine attributes. Although in today's society, much is made of how women can do nearly everything a man can do; men value women best for our differences, not the ways in which we are the same. Men appreciate women for our grace and beauty. Men enjoy our softness and see it as a way to be in touch with their tender side, a side they dare not show to other men. A hard-working woman is good to have on your committee. But when a man goes home, he'd prefer a loving partner to a hard worker.

It's not an easy transition for the modern Black woman to make. It sounds submissive, reactionary, even oppressive especially since we've had to fight so hard for so many things. We hear that the ratio of males to females is not in balance. We see men who have narrow and stereotypical views of women. We have known so many men who were shaky, slick and untrustworthy; yet, if we are honest with ourselves, we must admit that we are shaky, slick and untrustworthy in our own unique ways. Getting pregnant, for example, isn't all one person's fault. Two people play a part in what happens to a couple, good and bad. Even in situations that are favorable for mating and marriage, we still have a hard time. Not having a husband allows us the freedom to do whatever we want to do, when and how we want to do it. Having one means we have to share the power, and certain points will have to be surrendered. We begin to feel that the marriage, the relationship, the man is not worth all the work. But isn't there something wrong when we decide one-half of the human race isn't worth it?

We are terrified of marriage and commitment; yet, we dread the prospect of being single and alone. Throwing ourselves into a work of some kind seems to fill the void without posing a threat. However, like any other drug, the escape eventually becomes the cage.

To make the break, we need to do less and be more. I am learning how to *be still and know*, how to be trusting. I am learning how to stop competing with Black men and how to collaborate with them. To temper my assertive and aggressive energy with softness and serenity. I can examine my attitudes and those of women who are like me and see where we need to change. I'm not preaching a philosophy that *women should be seen and not heard.* It's just that I have seen that I - and many of my smart and independent sisters - are out of touch with our feminine center and therefore out of touch with our men.

About a year ago, I was at an oldies but goodies club. As a native Washingtonian, I love to do *the bop* and to *hand dance* - the dancing styles that were popular when I was a teen. In those dances, the man has his set of dance steps and the woman has hers. Partnered dancing allows for individuality, but the couple must still work as a team, and move as a unit. On this particular occasion, I was sitting out a record and watching the other dancers on the floor. There was enthusiastic abandon yet divine order - uniqueness yet unity - in their movements. What a wonderful gift it is to dance! In that quietly joyful moment a thought came to me: If a man were to say, "I'm going to lead and you're going to follow; I want you to adjust your moves to fit in with mine," I'd dismiss him as a Neanderthal. With my hand on my hip, I'd tell him that I have just as much sense as he does and that he can't tell me what to do. Yet, when on the dance floor, I love following a man's lead. I don't feel inferior because my part is different from his; I certainly don't feel I have to prove that I'm just as able to lead as he. I simply allow him to take my hand and go with the flow.

I am still single. I am over thirty and yes, a little bit scared. I am still a member of my church, have no plans to quit my *good government job*, and will continue to do what I can for my people. Those things will not change, but there are changes unfolding. Today I know that I have to bring some of that spirit of the dance into an intimate relationship. Now I'm learning how to relinquish control and sometimes follow a man's lead. Dancing solo - I've mastered that; today I can take my hand off my hip in order to hold the hand of a partner.

There is another side of my femininity beginning to flower that I had not even realized needed expression. I don't have to be a one-note feminist but a woman who can dance to the syncopation of multiple rhythms. It adds perspective to my thinking and balance to my politics. Getting back on the dance floor after a long absence feels awkward and a little bit frightening, but it feels good. Now I'm ready to accept change starting within me.

4

The Change Within

Grant me the listening ear, the eye that is willing to see...the mistake in what I thought was correct, the strength in what I thought was weakness.

-Howard Thurman

As I develop my listening ear, I find that there are huge regions of wisdom and motherwit that I am just beginning to explore. And most of that unexplored territory is within.

Too many of my attempts to change have been on the surface reaching out instead of settling down and reaching in. I have been putting new paint on a car that has a faulty engine. Today I am working to make changes from the inside out.

I have come to believe that it's more important, when confronted by relationship or friendship issues, that *I* change, rather than expecting my man or any other person in my life to change. As I begin to think and sense differently, the world around me begins to take a different shape. Doors that were shut, swing open. New and different people are drawn into my circle of friends. When the quality of change has been positive, then the quality of the men I attract is also positive. The inner character that I have developed, or

19

failed to develop, counts for as much as what he does in fostering a satisfying relationship. I can almost track my mental health by looking at the kind of man I was with during a given period in my life. When I have been less centered, the men I attracted reflected my imbalance. When my life has been more whole, the men I dated were more wholesome as well.

Centering down also includes developing that inner ear and trusting that inner voice. I have missed out on too many blessings by dismissing the thought that didn't seem logical, but later proved to be dead on the money. Not all wisdom is logical, straight-line, left-brain thinking. Not all battles are won by firepower and force. When I self-correct from within, I almost don't have to "do" anything on the outside. That sense of centeredness communicates itself to others without me having to speak a word. When I am communicating with my other, deeper voice, I know that God [my higher power] hears with His own listening ear and responds in a better way.

Four characteristics are necessary in order to strengthen our relationships with our inner ears: flexibility, balance, a willingness to be vulnerable and a tolerance for paradox.

Flexibility

Dancers have flexible bodies. They can bend, sway, and turn with ease. "We are not exercising, we are dancing!" calls out my African dance instructor when she sees that we are moving like wooden soldiers and not infusing our steps with energy and grace.

Traditional African dance is exuberant and energetic. It's as vigorous as it is graceful. A lot of African dance is done from a position known as the *plié*. A *plié* is when one's knees are bent. *Plié* comes from a term which means to bend or fold. African dancing requires flexibility and energy, resilience, and enthusiasm. To be able to bend one's knees gives more flexibility to the dancer and more spring and spirit to the dance.

Being flexible means you can bend without breaking. You can stretch and reach farther. You have grace under pressure. Listening to your inner ear is the same, especially when you sometimes hear exactly what you do not want to hear. It takes a lot of sweat, strain and tears to achieve flexibility; but once you learn how to balance, things become a lot clearer.

Balance

Hand-in-hand with flexibility is balance. Balance is finding and maintaining the mid-point between two extremes. In our interactions with men, it's important to be able to maintain our balance. I am not recommending silence over speech or being passive over being active, although those actions are sometimes necessary. There's a time to care and do for others, and there's a time for being benevolently selfish and taking care of ourselves. As an old rap record put it, "There's a time to sing and a time to shout and then there's a time to just chill on out." The wise woman will seek to utilize the best of both worlds rather than choose one to the total exclusion of the other. She will examine a situation and see what approach the circumstances call for. There are advantages in displaying traditional feminine behavior and there are advantages in being an independent woman. Seeking balance helps us bring two extremes into perspective and place ourselves in the position where we can benefit from each. The goal is not to only do one or the other, but to keep both in balance, even when it seems to be paradoxical.

Paradox

It is easier to keep both poles in balance when one has a tolerance for paradox. Webster's dictionary defines paradox as "a statement that seems contradictory, unbelievable, or absurd but that may be true in fact." It is this thinking that is reflected in statements such as" *In yielding, there is strength*" or "*You must stoop to conquer.*"

These concepts are often hard for me to embrace. A lot of times I want things to be black or white, yes or no, fight or flight. I find it hard to tolerate situations that are not "either-or," but rather "both-and." Yet when I am able to sit still in circumstances where I must tolerate paradox, I am usually rewarded.

In one of my jazz classes, the teacher was showing us a new dance combination; this one included leaps. When he did it, his body made a high and graceful arc up into the air near the ceiling; when I did it, my feet were sausages that flapped only inches above the floor. I wasn't the only one either. When he turned around to watch the class dance, he offered this word of advice, "To do a perfect turn, you must go down in order to go up."

Go down to go up. Another paradox. An interesting paradox. While I found that statement to hold much truth in my dance class. I was forced to recollect many of the events in my life where I have had to suffer pain to receive joy. I also observed that a runner at the starting block must rear back in order to spring forward. The bigger a building, the deeper into the ground the foundation must be laid. I found this statement to be very true in many areas in my life, but I also found out that it allowed me to be more vulnerable.

Acceptance of Vulnerability

Being well-defended might make good sense for an army, but from what I've seen it doesn't work too well for building relationships. Nobody wants their feelings hurt, but a degree of pain is inextricably linked to any pleasure. You can't dance all night without your feet hurting, and you can't have a baby without labor pains.

It feels dangerous to be willing to be vulnerable. However, being willing to be vulnerable is not the same as being a sucker. Being a sucker is behaving in a way you know to be foolish. Acceptance of one's vulnerability is acknowledging that you have weaknesses. But one also realizes that not acknowledging the fact of those weaknesses would be to put you at even greater risk.

The good news is that a willingness to admit our weakness, to reveal our wounds, to accept our vulnerability has its advantages.

Here's one small example, and again, it was on the dance floor that this idea crystallized itself for me. I had not been out dancing in months. I tried to get one friend after another to go out with me, but nobody was ever available. So finally I went by myself to the newest 'oldies but goodies' spot in town. I was a little intimidated, going to a club by myself, but I had a real desire to work off some stress. Dancing was the best way I knew how to do that. So I went alone.

I also went prepared. Since I didn't have a girlfriend to sit and chat with me while I waited to be asked to dance, I made sure I was dressed to thrill. I've got great legs, if I do say so myself, so I was wearing my highest heels and my sexiest skirt to make sure I was noticed. Well, I want you to know that for the first two hours I was there, no one noticed me. I sat nursing the melting ice from my 7-Up, and listening to oldie after oldie, while watching other couples jamming on the floor. After checking my watch two or three hundred times and stirring the empty glass with my straw, I decided that I would leave if my luck didn't change in the next thirty minutes. Soon after I made that decision, a man came over to my table and asked me to dance. We spent the rest of the night dancing and talking; I ended up having a very good time. Later, he told me that what drew him to me was the fact that I looked a little lost and lonely sitting over in the corner at the table all by myself. It was my vulnerability that achieved that goal for me, not my strength.

It seems sometimes that we don't ever want to relinquish our position of (supposed) strength. But not to relinquish, relax or retreat, at least some of the time, sets us up for greater wounding or defeat. I have observed a number of my single girlfriends who maintained that strong, impregnable persona - until they got pregnant. The very real, very vulnerable position in which pregnancy puts a woman suddenly melted that hard shell and they became much more accommodating. It was a rude awakening and an adjustment that brought a lot of emotional upheaval. That illusion of impregnability shattered. But rather than wait for an unplanned pregnancy or some other unexpected turn of events to come upon us, it's better to accept the fact that we are vulnerable in certain ways and it's necessary to relate to others in ways that accommodate the reality of our vulnerability rather than deny it exists.

Many of us are frightened by the idea that we may have to depend on others to help us get our needs met. It feels far more prudent not to need anyone, especially men. Yet, we feel disappointed when there is no man around to be of help. An acceptance of our vulnerability allows us to recognize that we do need others in our lives. In fact, knowing that we are vulnerable helps us to welcome others into our lives. "You have to look like you need people," said therapist Carolyn Lloyd, "Telling someone 'I don't need you. I got my own check...' You're defeating your own purpose of being cherished." Paradoxically, acceptance of our vulnerability is a strength.

Whatever aspect of femininity we find difficult to embrace, we must begin to own it and admit it is part of us. For those of us who are independent it means embracing the traditional woman within. For those of us who are sexually *liberated*, it means rediscovering that modest virgin. If we are religious, we may need to make friends with that street-wise-home-girl hidden inside.

We begin the change within by naming what is missing then seeking to bring it back. We become aware of what we are denying and bring it back to awareness. How can we tell what the missing piece of the puzzle might be? Take a look at the type of women you dislike. Chances are those women embody the parts of yourself that you are reluctant to claim. Whatever we need to invite and to integrate into our lives, it is an aspect that by definition has to feel different, uncomfortable, alien even. We will have to sing to a different tune, dance to a different beat. We must learn how to listen deeply. We will have to attune ourselves to new rhythms and move accordingly. However, we will still be able to use our feminine energy and strength to our benefit.

5

Feminine Energy, Feminine Strength

I'm a woman
  Phenomenally.
    Phenomenal woman
      That's me.

-Maya Angelou

One of my favorite oldies is "Do Right Woman - Do Right Man." "They say that it's a man's world, but you can't prove that by me," sings Aretha Franklin. "So as long as we're together, baby, show some respect for me." I say amen to that even though history does not seem to show evidence for any truly matriarchal culture, that is, one where the women dominated the men. In Carolyn Niethammer's *Daughters of the Earth* and Cheikh Ante Diop's *Two Cradle Theory*, we find that there have been matrilineal societies (where family ties are traced through the mother) and matrilocal societies (where husbands move to live with the bride's family) and even matrifocal cultures (where the role of mother is highly respected and revered), but never a human civilization where the women presided over the men.

So does that mean that women are destined to be powerless? Definitely not. Just because women are different, in some respects, doesn't mean that we are less. It doesn't even mean we are weaker. We are just different. And our differences are advantages, not liabilities. Rather than look at male and female as straight parallel lines that are the same but separate, I think of the sexes as undulating parallel lines, similar and complementary.

Magnetic & Dynamic Power

One of the ways that women and men can be different is in the expression of power. There are two ways to exert strength. One is through dynamic power, the other is through magnetic power. Understanding the contrasts between these two illuminating concepts was a realization that put many issues in perspective for me. Dynamic power is strength through doing. Dynamic people forge forward, use force, make demands, and see them satisfied.

Magnetic power is the power of attraction. It's a power that pulls, compels, and commands without speaking. It is the power of silence, coming into a deeper knowledge by listening to the unspoken messages. It is the power of the heart and ear over the head and hand. We need magnetic power. Magnetic energy is what places you in the right place at the right time. It's what operates when you stop turning over a problem in your mind and decide to sleep on it, and lo and behold, the next day you wake up with a good idea about how to solve it. It's what happens when the proverbial teacher appears at the very time the student is ready. Singers of this gospel song understand the workings of magnetic power.

> *That problem that I had*
> *It seems I could not solve*
> *The more I tried to work it out*
> *The deeper I got involved*
> *But I turned it over to Jesus*
> *And I stopped worrying 'bout it*
> *I turned it over to the Lord*
> *And He worked it out.*

Dynamic energy is good for interacting in the world. Dynamic energy gets things done. Dynamic women achieve on the job, get rules changed and bills passed, make their views known and their words heard - all without ever having to give up their feminine energy or feminine strength. Women, over the last 20 years have been acquiring and flexing their dynamic muscles. American women have greatly increased their presence in the labor force moving from 39% in 1972 to an estimated 47% by the year 2000 according to 1990 statistics from the National Commission on Working Women of Wider Opportunities for Women. Sixty-two percent of all African American women work. We have entered and excelled in fields that have been male-dominated for centuries. We need dynamic power.

In modern American culture, more value tends to get placed on dynamic power. Little emphasis is given to waiting, listening and being patient. We prefer speaking to listening, doing over being. Constant motion appears good; stillness, a waste of time.

When you bake a cake, there is a time for mixing, measuring, beating, blending, stirring and shaking. Then comes the time when you bake and wait. The actual baking of the cake is not done by the baker. While the cake is baking, the baker is waiting. Constantly opening the oven door, moving or shifting the pan, prodding or touching the batter all impede the cake's progress. The best thing for the cook to do at this juncture is nothing. Now is the time to be still and know that the power of the oven in conjunction with the nature of the cake batter will work together to bring something good to fruition.

When a case goes to court, there are many actions that take place leading up to the verdict. Motions are filed, jurors are impaneled, view points are argued, witnesses are cross-examined, facts are checked, and objections are raised, sustained, or overruled. Finally, the prosecutor rests his case. The defense rests her case. After all the machinations of the judicial system have stopped, then justice is decided. If the lawyers insisted on continuing to argue the case, a verdict could never be reached.

I have discovered that I have been short-sighted in acknowledging the quiet power of magnetic energy. It has been the missing ingredient that has prevented my success in numerous relationships. I have been constantly "testing the cake" when I should have been letting it bake. I have persisted in "arguing my case" when I would have been better served by resting my case. I have pursued a masculine and dynamic mind-set to solving certain problems that needed a feminine and magnetic approach.

Once I was losing an argument with a boyfriend because he could not see my point of view. As my anger increased, I felt the tears swelling up. I changed my tactics from winning the fight to getting him out the house before he could see me cry. Well, he refused to leave. He wanted to talk about it some more. I felt myself progressively losing control. I wanted to put this "Negro" out and then cry alone, consoling myself with the thought that "men ain't nothing, only Jesus understands. "What self-righteous self-inflicted deception! Finally, I couldn't hold the tears back any longer, and they just poured out.

"Now I've really lost," I thought. However, as soon as the tears appeared, the atmosphere in the room shifted. My man's hard line immediately softened. As I laid down my weapons and became vulnerable, he too stopped trying to control and became more willing to effect a truce. As we continued to talk in a more gentle and understanding way, I found my mind reeling. "What just happened here?" I wondered. "Had I known tears were such an effective ploy I would've used them long before now!" Then I had to check myself. This was not just a neat trick. It was my surrender, my letting go, my vulnerability that turned the tide.

I am not promoting winning through tearful intimidation as the way to manipulate your man. But this situation showed me that there is another way to win aside from the 'if you can't beat 'em, join 'em' school of thought. Before, I thought crying in front of a man was irredeemably weak. I was no helpless female. "I'm a strong, Black woman," I often told myself. I disdained the idea that any of the traditional feminine behaviors were valid or practical. Somehow I felt it unfair to use them. I thought of them as inferior - of little consequence. Although it worked for me, crying at work is not likely to be a wise move for everyone. However, in the domestic realm and in the choreography of intimate relationships, traditional feminine behaviors have impact and influence.

Power of the Feminine

What are traditional feminine behaviors? They are using subtlety and indirection as opposed to direct action and open confrontation. It is using a soft word instead of a sharp comeback. It is attending to the non-verbal communications as well as the verbal statements and listening to both with the third ear. The focus is on being rather than doing. Women value other women for our competence and intelligence - and so do men. But men also value women for our gentleness and beauty. When we include these feminine characteristics in our repertoire of behaviors, we only increase not diminish our ability to gain respect.

When I think of the word *lady*, Florence* is the type of woman who comes to mind. Florence was my supervisor and mentor for many years. We worked together in a women's advocacy organization. In addition to her responsible position, Florence was also a wife of over twenty years. Every day after work her husband would pick her up and greet her with a kiss at the car. Oftentimes I thought it amazing that he still kissed her hello after twenty years of marriage. I wondered what her secret was.

One of her secrets I surmised was probably her ability to know when to be assertive and when to rely on the more subtle, but equally powerful feminine approach in dealing with her husband. On one occasion, early in her marriage, she told me that she and her husband had gone shopping. When they returned home, he got out of the car. Florence remained in the car. He walked up to the front door of their home, and unlocked it. Florence remained in the car. He went in the

* denotes fictitious name

35

house. Florence remained in the car. Finally, it dawned on her husband that she had not yet come in, so he went back to the car. He graciously opened the car door for Florence, at which point she stepped out and they entered the house together.

"Didn't you fuss at him for not remembering to open the door for you?" I asked.

"Oh, no," she said. "I didn't have an attitude. I was very pleasant about the whole thing."

"Didn't you at least say something?"

"Oh, no," she said. "He understood my silence just the same."

Not every woman wants to have her car door held open for her. But a woman benefits from being accorded respect as a woman, in addition to whatever respect she commands as a person. A feminine modality can open doors that would otherwise remain shut, or which would have to be blasted down before they opened. Why curse at someone when being graceful is just as effective?

Being valued for our graces does not reduce us to mere ornaments or sex objects. It makes fellowship between the sexes more attractive and pleasant. It adds harmony to daily life.

Many expressions of feminine beauty point out the differences between woman and man. I have come to believe our differences are qualities to be enjoyed, not obstacles to be eradicated and overcome. One woman described her struggle to be Black and female as "...the right to be different and not be punished for it." I enjoy wearing dresses, pastels and bright colors. I enjoy polishing my nails. Although having to be concerned with my appearance is sometimes a nuisance (especially when it comes to dealing with my hair), it is also a way for me to celebrate being female.

Why is a feminine modality necessary? Why even is an alternative approach needed? What's wrong with being direct and straightforward? Well, human beings are complex and diverse. One size fits all is not true for pantyhose, much less human psychology. There are advantages in differences between the sexes (even as there can be discrimination based on the differences). No one person, or specialized group of persons, can do everything. It is recognition of this fact that accounts for the division of labor between males and females in most cultures. The burden for executing all of the important tasks of the tribe, nation or family does not fall on the shoulders of only one sex.

However, for many of today's Black women, we have become burdened with too many roles. We are expected to be dynamos at work and at home. We are mother and father to our sons and daughters; breadwinner and bread baker. We complain about the struggle of it all; yet, we also secretly enjoy being superwoman, taking a distorted pride in thinking we're in control. It's time to let go.

It seems dangerous and foolhardy to let go.

It's not practical, we say. Who's going to pick up the slack? To not stay in charge will mean, if not certain death, then definite failure.

I have long been more comfortable with the concept of God that's expressed in "God helps those who help themselves" than the concept of faith that says "Let go and let God." I feel more in control of the situation with the former. In the latter, I feel like I have no say, anything can happen - and it'll probably be something bad. God is supposed to be interested in my well-being, but hey, if I'm not taking an active hand in this thing, who knows what the outcome could be?

But there is a time and occasion for relinquishing control - or rather the illusion of being in control. I have discovered that a lot of my supposed faith is not actually faith in God, but faith in my own ability to marshal the necessary resources to pull myself out of a trap. If I don't fully trust God to help me without me taking the lead, then it's easy to see how I might refuse to accept the help from an average Black man. "He may interfere with my plans and prove more trouble than he's worth," usually follows that train of thought.

When I hear sayings like "in yielding there is strength," "the best way to keep what you have is to give it away," "to know that you do not know is best," and "you have to stoop to conquer," I am often baffled. It just does not seem logical. Yet it is a truth, a paradoxical but powerful and immutable truth. It requires faith to believe such a truth. It's a precarious and scary position to occupy. But faith motivated by love equals a position of strength.

One of the most well-known and dramatic examples of how surrender yields success comes to us from the scriptures. Two women appeared in King Solomon's court with a baby. Both women were roommates, and both women were prostitutes. Both women also claimed to be the mother of the newborn son.

"She rolled over in bed and crushed her baby just three days after he was born," said the first mother. "She got up in the middle of the night and switched her dead son with my son while I was asleep. When I woke up the next morning, I realized that the dead baby beside me was not mine."

"Not true," said the other woman. "It was her son that died. This baby is mine!"

King Solomon observed the women closely. He then turned his concentration to the baby's face. A fine son, but this infant's features were still too indistinct and unformed to determine a definite resemblance.

"Approach!" Solomon gave the order to the swordsman standing at attention nearby. "Divide the child in two and give half to each woman." Then the true mother of the living child cried out, "Oh, no! Don't kill him. Let her have the baby!"

This woman yielded. She surrendered her claim, relinquished her rights, did not exercise any of her assertiveness, she just gave up. If the story ended here we'd have to conclude that she had lost. But the story continues.

The other mother said, "Fine. Cut him in two and neither one of us shall have him."

At that point, Solomon ordered the sword resheathed and said, "The first woman, the one who asked that the child be spared - give the child to her. She is the mother."

The woman whose decision appeared weak, and destined for loss was the woman who prevailed. The woman whose decision wasn't aggressive or demanding but yielding and humble - that was the woman who got what she wanted. She was the woman who saved her life by "losing it" and saved her son's life as well.

I find it significant that the Bible, which is written with a very male-focused tone, personifies Wisdom as female. I think this is no error. Women, in order to be effective in their environment, must know how to couple knowledge with understanding. We must learn how to balance the left brain with the right brain. After all, not every situation is best handled by yielding. Feminine energy and wisdom are essential parts of the equation for health that is needed for the survival of our community.

Scheherazade

The power of magnetic energy, subtlety, feminine intelligence and creativity is illustrated in the story of Scheherazade and the tales of the Arabian Nights. This ancient Persian tale recounts one wise and imaginative woman who not only gained honor for herself, but brought spiritual healing to her man and salvation for her city.

The king, named Shah'ryar had a Queen whom he loved, but who was faithless. She cheated on him - with a slave, no less. Deeds done in the dark inevitably come to the light and when he discovered her sin he was filled with wrath, rage and revenge. Shah'ryar had the Queen and her lover beheaded. But even that did not satisfy him. He declared that from then on, every day he would take a new woman to be his bride. This Queen would be his royal partner - but only for one day. Come evening, she would retire with him to his chambers, but on the following morning she would be executed.

As the king decreed, so it was done. Daily he married and daily he executed the previous day's wife. Throughout the kingdom every household with daughters lived in anxiety and terror. Many families fled. All families feared.

Now this King Shah'ryar had an advisor known as the Wazir, whom he greatly favored. Because of his great affection for the Wazir, he had not asked for the hand of either of his two beautiful daughters. Although nothing of this arrangement was overtly spoken, the Wazir was very thankful to Allah and immensely grateful to the king for sparing his daughters. The eldest girl was an intelligent beauty, swift at numbers, learned in philosophy and poetry. She was especially gifted in understanding the psychology of men and she knew the ancient stories of her people.

One day this eldest daughter came forward and announced that she wished to marry the king. "To marry the King would mean your death!" exclaimed her distraught father. But she could not be persuaded otherwise. The king himself was more than willing to wed the Wazir's beautiful daughter but said, "Nevertheless, the decree stands and the day after the wedding will be her execution."

Before the wedding took place, the eldest daughter consulted her younger sister. "When I go to the King's chambers tonight, I will send for you. When you come you will find me telling him a story. Listen along with him in rapt attention and offer your enthusiasm for me to continue," she said, and her sister agreed.

So the ceremony was conducted; the marriage feast held, the day became night and the king along with his new queen retired to the royal bed chambers.

"Husband and Lord, might I entertain you with a tale?" she asked. "Yes, it would amuse me," he said.

And so she began an ancient fable - a thrilling tale with a handsome prince, a pretty maiden, magic, good and evil juxtaposed and the outcome... Well, she could not finish this story as the hour was late. "Oh, but the best part of the tale is yet to come!" exclaimed the younger sister.

"But alas, I cannot finish it tonight," replied the

elder girl, "and tomorrow ..."

To kill her the day after tomorrow would be just as good as to kill her tomorrow reasoned the king. And so, he spared her life an additional 24 hours that he might hear more of the story. But on the following night, the tale she spun was equally as enthralling, if not more so than the last and the King was compelled to stay her execution still another day, that he might hear more. And so it continued for 1001 nights. In the course of those thousand nights plus one, she bore him a prince, whom he loved.

"Surely you would not kill me and leave your prince motherless?" she said to Shah'ryar. "Surely I could not," he thought and slowly yet suddenly he came to himself realizing that he was wrong to exact revenge against all women based on the unfaithfulness of only one. Shah'ryar recognized that this clever and intelligent woman had risked her very life to impart to him this revelation. He came to know that he loved her, and not only he, but the whole of the city loved her. It was thus that she came to be known as Sheherazade, derived from "Shahr" and "azad", meaning "Savior of the city." The contemplation we endure during our single lives often enhances our married lives greatly.

6

The Single Life

It's natural to want to be married, and it's natural to want to be single. It's also natural to want to be both at the same time.

-Joy Jones

The single life. Many of us find ourselves living it, either by choice or by accident. And there are certain advantages to being single. (Just ask any married person you know.) Your time is your own, and so is your money. You don't have to check with anyone before you make a decision. You have far more discretion in choosing a course of action for yourself (and your children) because the needs and expectations of a husband are not there to influence or restrict you. I, too, have heard too many of my married women friends tell me how much they miss their single days and their freedom.

Freedom vs. License

There is a difference between having freedom and having a license - a marriage license, that is. It seems that signing a marriage license is like signing a contract giving up total control of your personal well-being. Freedom, on the other hand, is being able to control everything that you do, and all that you will allow yourself to come in contact with.

Writer Natalie Goldberg best expresses freedom by saying, "I used to think freedom meant doing whatever I wanted. Now I know that freedom is knowing what I'm supposed to be doing, and doing it."[1] We should also add that freedom is doing that which we know should be done, at the time we wish to do it.

The main difference between the realities of being single and being married is discipline. Being married requires discipline; it requires being able to compromise and listen to your partners rationalizations before making decisions.

Many singles have become undisciplined in such a way that we could never revert to the disciplined, calm person we would need to be to maintain a working marriage. This is not to say that we don't work hard. Rather, we expend a lot of energy and invest a lot of work pursuing actions that do not lend purpose, health or peace to our relationships. We fall prey to the "strong-Black-woman syndrome" and decide we don't need men. We may very well be strong, and we are certainly Black. But we do need men. I'm not asserting that women need men in order to give evidence of our worth, we need men simply because men and women all have need of each other.

We are clear enough about external goals and the means for reaching them. We have a five-year plan for work. We honor our pledges to help the church build a new wing. We refuse to tolerate racism. We are committed to caring for our children. But our men? We can take them or leave them. Who needs 'em? Divorce has become the modern rite of passage. Being single has come to mean being free.

A lot of us have negated the double standard, but what has it gotten us? The right to dutch treats, dangerous sex and families without fathers? It doesn't take a high IQ to see that it is unfair for men to sleep around and be praised for it, while a woman who does the same is impugned. But it is also not very smart for women to insist on indulging in behavior that is against our own best interests just because there are men who do it. The freedom to "do your own thing" without regard to how it impacts on the quality of our lives and the health of our community is an insidious form of self-destruction. Not every option is an opportunity.

~

One thing that struck me about some of the characters in Terry McMillan's popular *Waiting to Exhale* was their total lack of awareness of how their behavior caused at least a part of their bad luck. They had absolutely no clue as to what they should do - or should stop doing. So they continued to do what they had always done. In Al-

coholics Anonymous, they define insanity as doing the same thing over and over again, yet expecting different results. These women had the
freedom to do a variety of things - have sex,
change jobs, spend money. But they lacked discipline. Their actions only brought them repeated
pain and fleeting peace. Consistently repeating
the same dysfunctional pattern is bondage.

What is it we want our freedom to give us?
Do we want sex for sex's sake or as a feature of a
sane and satisfying relationship? We want better jobs - for what? To buy more shoes or to
strengthen our communities?

As we begin to know what we want and what
we should be doing, choices become framed
within a context. They cease to be fragmented,
unrelated, direction-less decisions. Many of the
old traditional roles for men and women did need
to be changed, and were stereotypical and rigid;
but they did provide a framework for what was
expected of partners in a relationship. Today we
have fewer stereotypes, less rigidity and lots of
change; but a frame of reference has been com-
pletely lost. As a result, many relationships have
been lost. It's preferable to have a rule, which is
then modified to meet the situation, than to have
no rules and think the resulting chaos is choice.

It is freeing when I can remember that the
larger purpose for being at my job is to be of
service to the people I work with and not just to
complete a certain set of tasks or to make a certain amount of money. When I can keep that

focus foremost, my mundane nine-to-five becomes a part of my spiritual journey and not a detour from it. When decisions have to be made, it is a little easier to make them because I can hold the conflicting alternatives up to the standard that asks, "How will this action serve others?"

I, like many of my peers, have had a harder time translating this into dealings with men. How can my actions be of service? How will my own needs be met? Is it my purpose to prove to men I'm just as "baad" as they are? Or is my purpose merely to be entertaining? Am I of greater service when I confront men? Is it my place to take anything they dish out? Where do I draw the line?

Being single is safe. We never have to test our ability to weather out the emotional storms and dull lulls of a committed, on-going, intimate relationship with a man. When you date, you can choose to be with the man, or not to be with him. When you're married, he's there all the time-like it or not.

Being single also gives us a free rein to complain about men. It's easy to blame our failures, our bad luck, our single state itself on the fact that those "shiftless men" just won't do right. If Black men would just do what they are supposed to be doing, then we wouldn't be in the fix we're in. Right? Yes, it's all their fault. Wrong!

Certainly Black men have been a part of the problem, as have White men, White women -

and Black women. We all have our shortcomings, contradictions and inconsistencies to face up to. We have refused to budge when we should have yielded, and yielded when we should have stood firm. We are even quick to check the exit signs as we enter a relationship, just in case we have to depart. Male-bashing is cheaper than renting a movie and more entertaining than a soap opera; it allows us to get away clean. When we toss in a few statistics about male crime, unemployment and drug addiction - who could blame us for blaming them?

Complaining about male shortcomings keeps the spotlight from focusing on us. We can avoid facing the woman in the mirror and seeing her shortcomings. After all, once we clearly face ourselves it is harder to pretend that there is no work for us to do to correct those shortcomings. Shining the spotlight on someone else is a clever way to delay serious self-examination.

There are also hidden, more subtle payoffs to being single. Once someone complimented me on looking younger than my actual age. "How have you managed to look so young?" I was asked. "By not having a husband and kids!" I quipped. Although I meant it as a smart remark, there is truth to the fact that family life is extremely demanding and takes its toll on a person both physically and mentally.

It's fine to be single. Nevertheless, there are those of us who are single and wish that we were not, despite all the reasons there may be for a single lifestyle.

We come by this desire honestly. The desire to mate and to marry is a strong and primeval force. In traditional African society, all adults married. Dominique Zahan writes in *Religion, Spirituality and Thought of Traditional Africa* that

> ...In Africa, celibacy is not viewed with any favor and ... men and women view marriage as the ideal human state in this world. This is so deeply rooted in the minds of Africans that single persons...find no excuse in their eyes.[2]

Sometimes these biological and social imperatives to marry (especially when divorced from a supportive spiritual or cultural framework) compel us so forcefully that we marry anybody rather than face the possibility of never marrying at all; and we almost always end up marrying badly as a result. Or, we forego the marriage trip and go straight for the baby, deciding that it's better to get at least a part of the family package rather than none of it at all. The result is to end up single after all is said and done, and usually miserable. But being single doesn't have to mean being miserable.

Receptive and Waiting

Coping with being single requires all the qualities mentioned earlier for good relationships: flexibility, balance, a tolerance for paradox, and a willingness to be vulnerable. And it also takes an attitude of receptivity to whatever life brings.

Receptivity means being open to possibilities. It means working on the spiritual and cultural links that will support us while we are waiting for our soulmate to find us. And it also means not-waiting, or at least not being in a mode of physically waiting without doing all else that needs to be done in the interim. We should not be anxiously, irritably, nor idly passing away the time. When we are not-waiting we have an attitude that is relaxed and receiving. We do not do desperate things to attract a man if one is not immediately appearing on the horizon. Although we want to cultivate our appearance, our knowledge and our feminine attributes, we do so for our own growth and not just to entrap a man. Otherwise, one becomes more of a predator than a potential mate.

Being the right woman is as important, even more important, as finding the right man. We are not waiting in the sense of standing by the phone hoping he will call. We still develop our inner resources and pursue outside interests.

"For the secret of waiting patiently is that, in fact, she does not wait, but persistently (though somewhat reluctantly) continues to invest herself elsewhere both personally and socially," reveals Dr. Toni Grant.[3]

Nearly all of my most satisfying relationships evolved during times when I wasn't really looking. Jerome showed up at a place in my life where I felt I needed to stop being so uptight, especially with money. I usually refused to buy anything unless it was on sale. That's not a bad policy, but I had a pretty miserly spirit. I love to read the newspaper but was too cheap to buy a subscription; I'd pick up a forgotten paper left on the subway train during my ride to work in order not to pay twenty five cents at the newsstand. One of the things I decided to do was enroll in a new dance class at a "real" studio with professional dancers and not just sign-up for the typical $4-a-session aerobics class. It was there that I ran into Jerome who I had known from a continuing education course that we had both been enrolled several years prior. When I ran into him at the studio and decided to speak, I wasn't on the make, or hoping to get lucky; I was simply being friendly to an old classmate. But two weeks later, we had our first date, and many more followed.

Most of the happily married people I know, both wives and husbands, did not find their partner as the result of a deliberate spouse-hunt. Those who, due to family expectations, pressure from friends, or their own desires and anxieties, decided it was "time to get married" or "I ought to settle down now" are the ones who have had the greatest disappointments with married life. For the more satisfied couples, marriage almost sneaked up on them and caught them unawares. It is another one of life's paradoxes of finding the very thing - or person - you're looking for once you quit looking.

Being receptive also means accepting reality. It means coming to terms with who we are and where we are right at this very moment. We don't succumb to the futility of a fantasy about the future arrival of an African Prince Charming. Nor do we sink in frustration about the fact that he is not here now. He may never come. It is for this reason that we must have developed a balanced inner life. It will be the richness and complexity of this inner strength that will sustain us as we wait at not-waiting. We will have developed something good on the inside that will recognize other good things and magnetize them to us - and that good thing may not be a man. Being receptive allows us to not resist healthy changes as they come along because they aren't what we think we want. Receptive women can discover, own and embrace many parts of the whole woman, even the aspects that seem foreign and feel uncomfortable. It means accepting the fact that life seldom works out precisely according to our preconceived plans and has a path and direction of its own.

That unplanned path or different direction is a good one, better than the one we had in mind, even if we can't see it when waiting to find out what will happen next. A period of waiting - often in the dark - is part of the process for every thing that grows. A seed lives in the darkness of the ground before becoming a beautiful flower.

A fetus waits in the darkness of the womb before becoming a beautiful baby.

But it's hard to wait for our change to come. Sometimes waiting takes more faith than working. It's easy to retreat into our favorite habits - overdosing on church, eating for entertainment, compulsive work, escaping with the latest bestseller or the newest mini-series on TV, or repeatedly choosing unavailable or unsuitable men as partners, thereby "proving" to ourselves once more the futility of it all.

Our cherished distractions and our constant busyness keeps our minds off the pain - but it also keeps our minds off of change.

Honesty and Change

Honesty is a good starting point for change. As I admit that maybe some of my own actions have contributed to my current state of being, I am more willing to consider changing some of those actions. This does not negate what others have done. It doesn't excuse racism or sexism. It doesn't mean that men are off the hook for the ways they have hurt, cheated or neglected us. It means we see that we have had a hand in shaping our own consequences. "I have never been confined," writes poet Mari Evans, "except I made the prison."

I have found that even as I have passionately sought wholeness, I have resisted it. Even as I eagerly pursue intimacy, I fear it. I go to the party

Between Black Women

wanting to dance, but am afraid to get out on the floor.

Oftentimes we say that the reason we are single is because there are no good men, no marriage-material men. Of the few available males, all are bad boys.

Sometimes we attract "bad boys" because it is a backhanded way of both keeping control and surrendering control. At some level, we are very much aware of the demands and sacrifices marriage requires. Who wants all that work? Yet we still long for love and companionship. So we go for the "bad boy" anyway. The man who is always in-and-out of work, the charming alcoholic, the man who is married or is in some other way unavailable justifies our attitude that "men ain't nothing" and satisfies our need for a limited amount of companionship. We are "in control" in the sense that the obvious unsuitability of this man guarantees that we will not have to commit to him in any significant way. And we gain a feeling of control and distorted pride because his weakness makes us appear so "together" by contrast.

Yet because he is such a bad boy, often someone with more street experience than what we have, his company feels virile, exciting, dangerous and makes us feel more feminine, excited and stimulated in return. Therefore, we are able to "let go" and "yield" in a very narrowly defined way.

I'm as guilty of this syndrome as the next

56

woman. Some time ago I found myself attracted to a married man. It is not my practice to date married men, so I was quite surprised - and alarmed - to find myself responding to his subtle - and not-so-subtle - suggestions, particularly since during that time period I was enjoying a season of attention and pursuit by several single and available guys. "Why do I waste my time thinking about this married man when I can do better?" I questioned myself. But in thinking back on it, I believe the very availability of the available men was a key factor in the appeal of the unavailable one. As I had begun to yield to a more magnetic kind of energy and my feminine qualities drew men to me, the dynamic woman in me began to feel scared. She reasserted herself by gravitating towards a situation where I could maintain that feeling of being free and single. Realizing this helped me to place him in the category of "just friends" and turn my attention to a more wholesome path.

Admitting to ourselves our own character faults becomes the first move towards a destination that can lead us towards integrity. With more honesty, we are more open to clearly seeing which paths bring us closer to our destination of personal freedom - and which paths will lead us away. We will not have to walk down every street we pass just because we have permission to do so. We don't have to jump to every beat just because we hear the music playing. We don't have to do everything men do just because we can. We can choose those tasks and perform those behaviors that lead us to become more fully the women who we really are, and leave all those other "options" alone.

Right Motive, Right Action

There are those of us who feel that we are "better" than everybody else and that our preferred status gives us permission to regard people with less respect than their due. The rules apply only to "them" - those poor unfortunate, unenlightened ones but not to "me" - I'm the one exception and the prime example. There are those who are too "holy" to share any interests with a "carnal" husband. There are the ones who have so much education, money or contacts that they are uncomfortable around brothers who are not "on their level." Then when our superior status fails to generate satisfying relationships, we are confused. Certainly we could not be at fault because we are mentally, morally, or materially so far above that than those "other" folks.

Staying Open

Instead of building distractions or trying to hold ourselves so high above the fray to wall out what we perceive to be painful issues, it is to our benefit to continue being receptive. Yes, receptivity is another one of those classic feminine traits that is currently not in vogue. Assertiveness rather than receptivity gets respect. Nonetheless, being receptive leaves one open for good things to come one's way. Being receptive allows one to suspend judgment for awhile before coming to a conclusion. It permits both poles of a paradox to co-exist and gives us more balance in our perspective. Being receptive affords the luxury of being able to select from the array of options brought before you rather than singlemindedly and one-dimensionally locking in on the narrow view you have predetermined as the only right course.

John S. Mbiti writes in *African-Religions-and-Philosophy* that "For African peoples, marriage is the focus of existence. It is the point where all the members of a given community meet: the departed, the living and those yet to be born."[4] For those of us who are single, we may not want to or be able to marry, but we still need to participate in the cycle of life that marriage represents. We may live a single lifestyle, but we can not live a separate lifestyle. The soloist still has to harmonize with the choir. We must strive to find ways to contribute to and connect with the community. Rather than be isolated from the coupled-off portion of the race, we can be single in ways that affirm our unity and continuity with the rhythm of life. One of the gifts of being single that we can give to the community is our availability. Those of us who are single usually have more availability and flexibility which we can use to help families and individuals in ways that they cannot help themselves. The average slave mother was probably too overworked and stressed to plan an escape for herself and her children. But Harriet Tubman was able to provide the way to freedom for whole families.

We may not need to lay our lives on the line in such a dramatic way, but there are still many ways we can be useful. When we give to our extended families and the greater community, we enlarge and deepen our own capacity to receive. As we become more open and more giving, we are able to receive more gifts and more blessings from life, maybe even that relationship we want. But even without it we can still have our needs met and live lives that are satisfying. A wise woman told me that everybody needs three things in life: something to do, someone to love and something to look forward to.

Being single doesn't preclude those primary needs from being met, but being closed-minded will. Whether we are single or married, it is important that we always seek to be positive images and maintain positive relationships.

7

Positive Images, Positive Relationships

We can say "Peace on Earth," we can sing about it or pray about it, but if we have not internalized the mythology to make it happen inside of us, then it will not be.

-Betty Shabazz

Who do you think you are? Who are you becoming? What is the story of your life? A large part of who we think we are and who we expect to become is formed by our cultural myths. By myths, I don't mean lies or stereotypes. Myths are the stories and belief systems handed down from generation to generation. They are images, themes and symbols that are enduring and recurrent.

Our relationships, to a large degree, are shaped by our images of what is a "good" woman, the "right" man, a "happy" family. Often those myths by which we shape our thoughts and behavior are so unconscious that we give them no thought. We absorb them as truths and blindly accept their consequences. What are some of the stories and images that are popular in our culture, and how do they influence our relation-ships?

One of the contemporary themes among Black folks seems to be that of the strong, independent, Black woman. Every February, we hear stories about Sojourner Truth and Harriet Tubman, even many of our popular literary pieces and newspaper headlines trumpet Black women who have made it without men. I know my own parents emphasized to me the importance of getting a good education and a good job "so that I wouldn't have to depend on any man." That advice was good then, and it is still good advice today, but I was never told how to make it with a man. I have single-lifestyle survival skills, but what skills work for coupling? Who do I look at for role models? The only variation on the "strong, independent, Black woman" theme is the "He-done-me-wrong" syndrome. When there are problems in a relationship we believe it's the man who is at fault - after all, we "know" how trifling men are. Intellectually, we understand that both the woman and the man play a part in creating troubles. But emotionally, we feel he's the only one to blame. I did myself a great deal of damage by believing in this particular cultural myth.

Some years ago, I went in for a routine gyne-cological exam. The clinic doctor told me I had fibroids and that it would require surgery to have them taken out. "Fibroids? What are fibroids?" I asked the doctor. "Whatever they are, ain't nobody cutting on me!" I exclaimed to myself.

Fibroids are benign tumors that grow in the uterus. The exact cause of fibroids is unknown, and there is no known prevention method. Some say they occur more frequently among African American females, although they are very common among all women.

My fibroids didn't grow rapidly at first, but over a five-year period they grew to the size of a four month old fetus. There would be dormant periods, then periods where they would dramatically increase in size. As the months passed, I did a great deal of reading about women's health. I came across a book that changed my thinking about my condition and how to treat it. This book listed a variety of physical illnesses and the emotional and mental attitudes that the author believed to cause them. Under fibroid tumors, I read "a blow to the feminine ego."[1] Medical science may not have a clue as to what causes fibroid tumors, but that explanation made plenty of sense to me. My tumors had appeared as an important love relationship had ended, and the periodic spurts of growth corresponded with every attempt I made to resume contact with that man. I had that "he-done-me wrong" attitude, which put all the blame on him. But my bad attitude didn't hurt him; it hurt me. Literally and figuratively, it tied my guts in knots.

I know I feel much more comfortable believing in the image of a God who helps those who help themselves, rather than in the image of a Higher Being who asks me to "let go and let God."

With the former worldview, I feel like I have more control; God may be in charge, but at least I can act as my own consultant. God and I are working this thing out together. If things go well, it will partly be due to my own efforts; God will have to share the credit with me - or so I like to think.

On the other hand, if I let go and let God - I have no control in the matter. I have surrendered. I have said to God: "Not my will but Thine be done. You're the Choreographer, I'm just following Your steps." It gave me great fear to consider this kind of faith. Suppose God did something I didn't like. God had already allowed my man to leave me. Could God really be trusted?

Images of Illness, Images of Health

I dreaded the idea of surgery because the usual method for treating fibroids is undergoing a hysterectomy. I did not want a hysterectomy. I cried. I prayed. I pulled out all my "strong Black woman" armor to fight this thing. During one occasion when I was praying about the fibroids, I found myself thinking aggressively about the situation - "I command these tumors to leave my body in Jesus' Name; I condemn this terrible condition that has come upon me" - I was constantly praying. But soon after I started, I heard that still, small voice urging me to "love yourself better." Love? I certainly thought I already loved myself, but to show love in the midst of this condition? Love? What I thought needed strength, attack and warfare required only love?

Even with my change in awareness, I still had to have surgery. But my research turned up the option of having a myomectomy rather than a hysterectomy. The myomectomy is an operation that allows only the tumors to be removed, leaving the uterus intact. Most doctors don't want to be bothered doing a myomectomy; it's a complicated, difficult operation. Hysterectomies are easier to perform. But I found a female African American surgeon who was willing to do the procedure. Yet even she cautioned me that there were no guarantees. Once the operation was underway, if she felt it necessary to do a hysterectomy, she would do so. I had to grant her permission in advance to conduct the surgery as she saw fit. Once I was placed under anesthesia, I would not know the outcome until it was all over.

I had done all I could do. My dynamic energy had empowered me to seek useful information, to evaluate and reject various doctors, while my magnetic energy had opened my mind to revelation in prayer and insight about my feelings. I had done all I could do. Now was the time to surrender to God and accept His results.

I'm happy to say that surgery went smoothly, the 26 fibroids were removed and no hysterectomy was done. Illness came as a result of a flawed mythology. Healing came as I changed my personal mythology. As I changed the quality of the stories I told myself about my life, I improved the quality of my life.

Good Mythology, Good Relationships

What are the stories you tell yourself about yourself? What are the stories we tell to one another to explain why things unfold the way they do? What images do we carry when we relate to one another?

Thoughtful members of the African American community are concerned with promoting positive Black images - and rightly so. Some situation comedies, evening news broadcasts and a whole host of TV crime shows would give the impression that black folks are all fools or crooks. The predominance and popularity of these images subtly color our own views of ourselves, even though we know intellectually that it's a distorted picture. Story and image are powerful and they imprint without the permission or active participation of the intellect. There are Black folks who pay bills on time, maintain their families and who are not on drugs. There are Black men who cherish their wives, and Black women who love their men. We don't hear about these quiet doers as often as we'd like or as often as we need to. We vitally need to tell and to hear those stories.

It's been hard to identify many stories that celebrate flourishing Black family life and couples who succeed. I find this frightening because in many respects it is hard to become something if you have never seen it. Because our knowledge of our history is sketchy, we only celebrate a few personalities and they are better known for their endeavors in the public arena rather than for success in their domestic life. We know little of the coping skills that allowed Amenhotep III and Queen Tiy of Egypt, King Menelik and Empress Taitu of Ethiopia or Bill and Camille Cosby to have enduring marriages.

At this time in current history, where so many marriages are in trouble or failing, it becomes even more imperative to have a cultural mythology that provides examples of how to live. "You can't develop a relationship without a strong foundation and a good mythology," states social worker Money Helton. When we can't look to our immediate circle of peers and superiors for an example of what to do, we must rely more on the cultural mythology to provide role models, signposts and direction.

Renowned educator, Jawanza Kunjufu points out that

> we hear more about Frederick Douglass, than about his colleague, Martin Delaney. More about Jesse Jackson than Louis Farahkhan. More about Martin Luther King than Malcolm X. In the former, these men sought more mainstream involvement with Whites than the latter, who supported a more separatist or nationalist philosophy.[2]

In American and European literature of

historical women, we read about women who, although achievers in their own right, were also successfully married. In addition to learning about Susan B. Anthony, Joan of Arc, Helen Keller and Mother Theresa, we also study Abigail Adams, Madame Curie, Betty Ford and Eleanor Roosevelt. By contrast, in Black literature, we read primarily of women who were achievers in the public arena, although their family life was short-lived or non-existent. We know more about Harriet Tubman than about William and Ellen Craft, the slave couple who gained their freedom by working together and trusting each other. More press seems to be given to Tina Turner, who has prevailed despite her stormy relationship with Ike, than to entertainers Ashford and Simpson, who have not only managed to maintain a stable marriage, but who manage their own business as well.

What could be the reason for this trend? As with the list of Black heroes, perhaps it is more in the interests of the main-stream culture to promote an image of Black women going it alone, rather than in solidarity with men. By internalizing a rugged individualist ideal, we become easier to manipulate, and easier to keep divided. After all, the slave woman who could readily adjust to and even take pride in her ability to do without a man could get back to work more easily than the one who felt something essential had been lost. I suspect the same dynamics are in force relative to modern Black working women who still serve the workforce as a non-threatening and cheap supply of labor.

Community and Connectedness

A significant part of our healing includes recovering our historical icons of healthy family and community life and creating new ones where necessary. We need myths that give us images of community and connectedness. Money Helton emphasizes that we need *a clear understanding of who developed the universe, who created people and put them on this earth.*

One of the prominent ideas in Christian religious mythology is that of salvation being a personal and individual transaction. The belief that if only one person existed in the entire world - me - that Jesus still would have sacrificed his life in order to save me and me alone. I believe that is true. But I also believe in another view of salvation. God is not only interested in saving isolated individuals, but in redeeming whole households, nations, communities. In the Old Testament, God is about the business of saving the entire nation of Israel, not just a particular person, here and there.

I'm sure that when Christianity was taught to the slaves, it wasn't in the interests of the slavemasters or the missionaries to tell stories that showed that God desired to deliver a whole race out of bondage. But they could safely tell those stories that gave hope for a personal deliverance based on one's individual relationship to God.

It's desirable, and it's necessary; it's imperative to have a personal and saving knowledge of God. But I think African Americans also need that corporate sense of salvation. We long for that spiritual sense of community where we know that our lives are interwoven with the lives of our friends, neighbors, cousins, co-workers, children and lovers. We need that connectedness that was the daily reality in the African village, but which is only an occasional occurrence in American cities. I was amazed to learn that

> in every city where Martin Luther King conducted a march, crime in the Black community went down. Even in recent times, when Nelson Mandela conducted his tour of the United States in 1990, crime went down in each of the cities he visited.[3]

What a beautiful example of how a true story of hope, honor and triumph triggered in us a very tangible expression of how we can treat ourselves better; how we can love each other better.

Beliefs We Live By

The word "belief" derives from a term which means "by-life" or "to live by." Our beliefs are the stories we live by. If we believe that our men are hopeless and that women are stronger or superior to them, then we will live our lives in a way that supports that erroneous belief.

We need to evaluate and change the stories we tell ourselves. We must re-examine our my-thology. In order to transform our lives we must transform the stories we tell about our lives.

Without a vision (the scriptures teach us), the people perish. But even with a distorted vision, the people will perish or at the very least, de-spair.

Part of the prescription for healing our rela-tionships is re-evaluating what we believe. What is our conversation like among each other? Do we carry the worldview of the at-large society into our talks over the kitchen table, our coffee break chats, our conversations on the telephone?

It's time to balance the horror stories with the healing stories. Uncover and recount the stories of Africans and of African Americans who have worked collectively. Don't only talk about the "he-done-me-wrong" stories, but also the occa-sions when "he-done-good." Publicize the story about the woman alone who succeeds against the odds, but also publicize the couple who joined together to achieve a common goal. We may get titillated by Phil's or Oprah's shows about "women who hate men and the men who love them" but we also have to demand equal air-time for programs about families who are making it.

As we examine, and then change, the mythol-ogy we believe about ourselves, we ourselves will change. Our third ear will become more at-tuned and in turn will stimulate the rest of the soul and the body to follow the call. We will be able to hear and respond to other members of the community more readily - and they to us. We will be able to know when to sing harmony when that is needed, or when to take the lead when that is required. We will know when to remain silent.

The power of myth and story can be the cue for the healing process to unfold. With new stories to tell we will hear the dire news about the black family with a new ear. We will hear the still, small voice that will instruct us how to self-correct. We will "hear" our vision more clearly.

Without a vision, the people perish. With a vision, the people flourish. But is a vision enough to survive a crisis?

8

Cooperation in the Face of a Crisis

A good thing has happened in the African American community. Words and phrases like EMPOWERMENT, RESPONSIBILITY, IMPROVING SELF-ESTEEM have all become part of our vernacular.

-Dr. Ingrid D. Hicks

While talking to group of sixth grade girls about their goals, I requested that they "imagine they were twenty-five years old and tell me what their lives would be like then." As each girl in this class of twenty responded, only one envisioned a husband in her future. One girl said she wanted to be a teacher and that she wanted support for her children. I wasn't sure if by "child support" she meant school supplies and materials for the children she would teach or a check to provide for her own offspring; she meant the check. No mention was made of a husband or even a steady boyfriend, just children and a check to support them. The idea that a man might be wanted or needed to provide something other than money was not a factor for consideration in her equation for family life.

To be sure, males in our community can be rightly regarded as an endangered species as the result of racism, poverty, as well as the self-destructive acts that they perpetrate upon each other. Yet I don't think that gives us permission to also think of the Black man as an invisible man.

These attitudes are just one reflection of our distorted views of ourselves and our relationships to the other sex. The Black family has approached the crisis stage. A few of these crises are:

~ The chance that a child will experience poverty increases to 90% if he or she lives in a family headed by a single woman under the age of thirty. (*Young, Black & Male in America* by Jewelle Taylor Gibbs, 1988)

~ Forty-seven percent of Black teens have had intercourse, 27% of Hispanic teens, 24% of White teens. Those who do not plan on college are more likely to have sex. (Planned Parenthood-Harris Poll, 1987)

~ Beginning in 1980 - for the first time in our history - female-headed families with children outnumbered married couples: 1960 - 78% of all Black families were two-parent families.
1970 - 64%
1980 - 48%
1985 - 40%
(State of Black Family, 1990)

The only way to resolve these crises is through rebuilding social and family relations. And I believe these relationships, particularly male-female relationships, can only be salvaged through an attitude of cooperation. The notion of cooperation and collectivity is not a new one. The traditional West African mindset is one of individuals willingly working for the good of the whole.

Although we frequently talk about embracing that African modality, our day-to-day behavior sometimes betrays us. When I am on the phone talking with my girlfriends, it sounds perfectly reasonable to say "A man can't do anything for me. I can do bad all by myself." But when I hear those attitudes reflected back to me from the mouths of children, then I realize how distorted and possibly destructive those attitudes can be.

A few years ago, a third grade teacher told me she was trying to impress upon her students the need to take school very seriously. To drive home the point, she recited to them some of the dire consequences brought about by a lack of education. One of the statistics she cited was the fact that few Black men attend or graduate from college.[1] Sixty percent of all African American college students are women. She also mentioned the appalling large numbers of Black men who are in prison. To her horror, the girls in the classroom began cheering.

"Yaay!" the girls shouted gleefully. "The girls are better than the boys! The girls are better than the boys!" Somehow the young females in this class interpreted this dismal fact about Black males as a plus for them. They did not see a connection between their own fates and the destinies of Black men.

The attitude that our men are dispensable or somehow unconnected to us is not just the childish concept of young girls. We adult women often have an alarming "who needs 'em" attitude. Consider this excerpt from a response to a Black male columnist who argues that 1) much of what has gone wrong in America stems from the deterioration of the family and 2) that one reason for the deterioration - particularly in the low-income Black community - is "that Black boys learn tragically early to view themselves as expendable." A female reader wrote back to discredit his view stating:

> Daily, Black women attempt to avoid, even flee, situations in which they are demeaned, belittled and stripped of their dignity and humanity. In truth, if the Black American community is to survive, Black women and girls must learn trades and skills which will enable them to become healthy, independent, self-respecting competent individuals. What should be done to cause/enable Black men to become intelligent, responsible, supportive, desirable family members? I don't know, and really don't care.[2]

Dr. Toni Grant comments that one of the "big lies" of feminism is the idea of total self-sufficiency, that modern women don't really need men for much at all. She writes,

In this past decade, however, it has not been uncommon to hear contemporary women refer to men as 'studs,' in other words, good for nothing more than mating and breeding. And often, when I ask a modern woman exactly what she needs a man for, 'breeding' seems to be her primary answer.[3]

The idea that the active involvement and co-operation of a man is superfluous, unnecessary, optional in today's family seems to be a current cultural myth. Dr. Marion Secundy, a professor of medical ethics at Howard University College of Medicine and a social worker who operates a small private practice in Washington, D.C. shared how these attitudes get inculcated in African American females of all ages and then becomes a self-fulfilling prophecy.

This business of you can make it by yourself, Black men are no good and you don't need them, and variations thereof and [other] put-downs - we all know we've heard it - and said it. The implications of those kind of socialization messages... We program ourselves in such ways that we become so independent that we don't need them, and then they become burdensome to us.

Once again, there is a paradox to be managed, for after all, one does want young women to be independent and not at the mercy of dysfunc-tional men, yet able to cooperate with men when appropriate and to establish mutually supportive bonds.

"You want your daughters to be able to survive in case they don't have [husbands]," stressed Dr. Secundy, but we also want our daughters, our sisters and ourselves to be able to maintain a cooperative relationship.

So what kind of cooperation do women and men need to cultivate? It is an attitude of cooperation that understands the need for adherence to traditional sex roles - when appropriate - and when to utilize a more flexible and non-traditional approach.

Haki Madhubuti writes in *Black Men: Obsolete, Single, Dangerous? The African-American Family in Transition.*

> ...Enlightened education requires that gender distinctions be minimized to those areas where such distinctions are vital and necessary. Understand that I am not pushing for a gender-free society but a society where one is not oppressed due to sex, race, or religion. It is obvious that women *cannot* be replaced as mothers, nor men as fathers without serious and often detrimental disruptions of family....The one institution that a "developing" or "oppressed" people cannot do without is family. Non-functioning families produce nonfunctioning people.[4]

I once attended a lecture by Josef Ben Jochanon, known to his followers as Dr. Ben. Dr. Ben is an historian and Egyptologist who has done extensive study on the presence and contributions of

Black Africans in ancient Egypt (Kemet) and throughout the continent and the diaspora. Dr. Ben is also an atheist, but at this particular lecture he made a comment that I found deeply spiritual. He said, "The real holy trinity is you, your mother and your father."

I find this statement important and provocative because it underscores the fact that when the male and female principles are not in concert - when one is missing - a spiritual crisis results.

It also makes the spiritual practical. Mother, father, child. Negotiating these relationships is the foundation for a truly centered, spiritual life. To be able to build and sustain functional man-woman, parent-child or even sister-brother bonds is a better measure of spiritual fitness and attainment than church attendance or career success. Even if we are not in marriages or do not have children of our own, we can be supportive of those who do, and act as members of the community that live a lifestyle worthy of emulation.

Memorizing a million Bible verses has it's place, but it pales behind the very real accomplishment of knowing how to get along with people. Scripture itself even points out - "How can you claim to worship God, whom you have never seen, when you can't get along with your neighbor whom you see daily?" Our spirituality needs not only to be ritual, it also needs to be practical. Practical ways to implement better family interactions are fairly plain and straightforward.

One suggestion comes from educator Jawanza Kunjufu who suggests that we find out what kinds of things folks did to entertain themselves prior to the invention of the radio and TV - and do those things. Things like play musical instruments, sing together around the piano, play games where both the adults and the children participate together.

And yes, there are African American families who actually do things like that. The extended Spriggs family of Arlington, Virginia, a Washington, D.C. suburb, is noted for their devotion to church and music. "We always had a piano in the family!" said one of the older women in the clan. "We had a lot of fun. We could entertain ourselves."

Singing around the piano and teaching piano lessons to one another sounds corny, but it's remembered fondly by this woman and it continues to be a bond that knits family members together in a way that retreating beneath a set of headphones or becoming visually paralyzed by the TV can never do. It fosters communication and self-expression plus this informal family give-and-take often extends the circle of blessings beyond the immediate family to the whole community.

In the case of the Spriggses, they put their talents to use to help raise funds for their church, Calloway Baptist Church. They had nineteen members of the clan performing all kinds of religious music from Panis Angelicus by Cesar Franck to "Tell Them I'm a Child of God" and other Negro spirituals. And they played to a packed house because as one observer commented, "Everybody was so amazed that we were able to get a whole family together to sing. They all thought it was beautiful." The yearning for community and cooperation among each other reveals itself to us periodically, as does the ways in which it can be satisfied. Remember how during each of Martin Luther King's marches, crime in the African American community went down. I believe that when charismatic leaders bring a message of hope and of unity, we listen and respond in like manner. Men and women both have the need and the desire - perhaps unconscious - to move forward cooperatively. We only need to work at making that coopera-tive forward movement conscious and consistent. And we don't have to rely solely on charismatic leaders to do it for us.

Efforts in that direction are already apparent. An increase in the institution of rites of passage programs for girls and boys are a reflection of that. It is recognized that young females and young males need serious and specific guidance in order to evolve into responsible women and men who regard their developing sexuality and their adult roles with respect and responsibility. They must understand that they have a responsi-bility not only to themselves or their immediate family, but to the larger clan and to society. The benefits don't just accrue to the young folks, either. It is satisfying to return some of the good that was freely offered to you. As another spiritual paradox tells us, "The best way to keep what you have is to give it away."

Another thing that has empowered the community is the increasing participation of African Americans in Kwanzaa, a fairly new holiday. Kwanzaa was started in 1966 by Maulana Ron Karenga. It is observed every year during the seven days between December 26th and January first and is modeled after the harvest festivals celebrated by many African peoples on the continent and throughout the diaspora. Kwanzaa emphasizes seven principles for living, or Nguzu Saba. These principles are: Umoja which means unity; Kujichagulia - self-determination; Ujima - collective work and responsibility; Ujamma - cooperative economics; Nia - purpose; Kuumba - creativity; and Imani - faith.

Individuals and couples who are able to live these principles in an on-going, daily fashion - whether or not they specifically observe Kwanzaa - are people who have a foundation for success. Living these principles, however, is not a fad or the latest thing to do in the Afrocentric set. Building relationships with an attitude of cooperation can be found among successful African American families throughout our history. A stellar example of this is found in the lives of William and Ellen Craft.

William & Ellen Craft

Ellen was a slave on a Georgia plantation. The offspring of an African slave woman and that woman's owner, Ellen looked nothing like her mother but was an exact replica of her dad. She was so similar in appearance to the master that she was sometimes mistaken as one of the children of the master's wife. As one might guess, Ellen was despised by the mistress of the house and was treated accordingly. Eventually the slavemaster's wife found a way to rid of this constant reminder of her husband's infidelity. She gave the 11-year old Ellen to a cousin living on a large farm near Macon. It was wrenching for young Ellen to be separated from her mother and familiar surroundings, but the move offered the possibility of a less vindictive owner.

It was at this new plantation that Ellen met William Craft. William's trade was that of a carpenter. But his primary work was not on the farm but in the city as a cabinet-maker. He was more fortunate than the typical slave in that he was allowed to keep a small amount of his earnings for personal use.

When William met Ellen, he fell in love with her. But Ellen was reluctant to marry. Marriage meant babies and her own experience had shown her that slavery had no regard for bonds between husband and wife, parent and child. She sought some way to ensure the protection of her future family. The only way that could happen would be to gain her freedom.

For months she and William tried to come up with schemes to free themselves, but no workable plan presented itself. Finally, they decided to commit to each other anyway and marry, but in William's words,

> at the same time ever to keep our dim eyes steadily fixed on the glimmering hope of liberty and earnestly pray God mercifully to assist us to escape from our unjust thralldom.[5]

It was in December of 1848 when an idea for escape came to William. And an inspired and timely idea it was, too. A mere one week and one day after he conceived the plan, William and Ellen were in safe hands in the free state of Pennsylvania. This was the plan. Ellen, being very fair, would disguise herself as a white man, an invalid, traveling by train to Pennsylvania to seek treatment from a specialist. William would accompany her as her slave. To hide the fact that Ellen could not read or write, she bound her right arm in a sling. That way she could ask others to sign her name when necessary and it would provide a ready excuse should someone wonder why she carried no book or newspaper on the long ride. Plus, it added credence to her invalid story.

It was a formidable undertaking. It required traveling 1000 miles through Dixie to Pennsylvania, the nearest free state and if captured, punishment would be severe and unmerciful. "I think it is almost too much for us to undertake," said Ellen when her husband presented the idea, "however, I feel that God is on our side and with his assistance, not withstanding all the difficulties, we shall be able to succeed."[6]

December proved to be an opportune month for an escape. At Christmas time, plantation owners gave their slaves time off and passes to visit family members on neighboring farms were more readily granted. If a slave was missing, his or her absence did not draw suspicion. Because William had saved some of his meager earnings, he was able to buy train tickets for the two of them and a pair of men's trousers for Ellen. The rest of her costume, she sewed herself.

So, equipped with disguise, small funds, a mountain of fear and a mustard seed of faith, they set off. The first obstacle met them at the train station. Of course, they could not sit together - Ellen was in the white section of the train, William relegated to the colored car. While gazing out the window of the car before departure, William noticed the cabinet-maker to whom he was hired out. The cabinet-maker was asking questions of the ticket-seller and even went through some of the cars inspecting the passengers. William hid his face and slid down in his seat and was passed unnoticed.

Meanwhile, Ellen found her seatmate to be one Mr. Cray, a man who was an old friend of her owner's family and who had known Ellen since childhood. She feigned deafness as a means to avoid conversation with him.

And these were not the only close calls. One white military officer criticized Ellen for speaking to William in a polite fashion advising her that "The only way to make a nigger toe the mark...is to storm at him like thunder, and keep him trembling like a leaf."[7] William was even chastised by one white man, an abolitionist, who considered him foolish for not deserting his "master" after offering him the means to do so.

Nevertheless, on Christmas morning, 1848, just eight days after the idea had come to mind, William and Ellen Craft were standing on free soil.

Quite a dramatic and inspiring true story from history. But their example has lessons for contemporary couples. First, this remarkable pair appear to have had a knowledge of their own self-worth. Despite the hell and hardship of chattel slavery, they had a vision of themselves that was not defined by their circumstances. They believed themselves worthy of a fuller living experience. They had a spiritual foundation that allowed them to define themselves as more than just slaves and they developed this sense of self-worth without advice from a pop-psych bestseller or years of therapy. It seems that contemporary approaches to problem-solving provoke us to do something, anything, just so long as we are busy "doing." We will take any action to distract ourselves from the pain. The Crafts had a plan of action, but it developed out of a plan of being first.

I can only imagine that they got this spiritual

grounding through the practice and celebration of Christianity as it was revealed to each of them in the development of each partner's personal relationship to God. The record doesn't state what version of Christianity was preached on their particular plantation, but frequently then, as now, religion was a Sunday morning drug to dull human spirits enough to allow people to endure another week of work. The Crafts managed to achieve that elusive but winning ratio of prayer, action and common sense that allows humans to do more than just exist, but to flourish.

My second point is not directly stated by Ellen Craft, but can be inferred by her actions - that is the willingness to delay gratification, specifically sexual gratification. William and Ellen Craft did not enter into marriage casually. As the vows state, marriage is "not to be entered into ill-advisedly or lightly but reverently, discreetly, advisedly and in the fear of God." Ellen, in particular, was quite reluctant to marry and from this I surmise she probably exercised sexual restraint. She was clear on the issue that to have a baby while still under bondage would be to place both mother and child at risk. She realized that, in this case, setting limits would expand her opportunities. It also seems apparent that Ellen and William took time to know one another before they "knew" each other in the Biblical sense. They evidently had talked to and trusted each other enough to learn they shared common values in their religious beliefs and most importantly in the goal of seeking freedom. For them, marriage was not merely the next move once the singles scene got tiresome. Marriage represented a commitment towards building a future together and a shared vision of what that future should be.

Finally, the couple seemed flexible in their attitudes about sex roles. It was William's idea for the scheme; he gave the lead. Ellen fulfilled the traditional role of following her man's lead, even though she had to execute the harder part of the plan. Yet she recognized that to refuse to shoulder the burden, although not fair in the limited view of the situation, would not serve her in the long run. After all, to refuse to do it would leave her in slavery. Sometimes I think today we fail to examine how our individual actions figure in the broader context. Sometimes what is "tit-for-tat" fair in the short term, shortchanges everyone over the long run.

But Ellen was not her husband's helpless little lady. She literally assumed a man's role, in both actions and appearance. Taking on the identity of a wealthy white planter can certainly be considered a very non-traditional job for a black woman slave. To facilitate the plan, William played servant to his wife. These two understood the need for flexible thinking in the execution of sex roles and were not fixated at one extreme or the other. They discerned when it was appropriate to behave by the traditional standard and when it was not.

Ellen and William did not conclude their adventure with a quiet domestic life in obscurity. They joined forces with Northern abolitionists and became active in the community of their new home, Boston, where they were able to empower others. They were so active, that word of their adventures filtered back to Georgia and bounty hunters were dispatched to capture them. On short notice, they fled to England, where they lived until the end of the Civil War and eventually made their permanent home back in Georgia.

William and Ellen Craft's story had a happy ending. But what if Ellen had said "Negro, you crazy?" when her husband first proposed the plot. What if Ellen had said, "It's not fair that I have to do the hard part?" What if she had not been willing to follow her man's lead when that was needed or to play the leading role when that was required? What if she had said "I don't believe in all that God stuff?" Or if she had said "I'm just going to be a-hoping and a-praying that Jesus will fix it by-and-by..."

The circumstances in which African American women and African American men find themselves today are certainly no worse than those of William and Ellen Craft. Yes, we must contend with racism, stressful family relationships, limited finances and imperiled communities. But I continue to believe that for every problem there is a solution. We can not meet these challenges in isolation, we must do it in relationship to one another. We need cooperation in the face of these crises. Working together, William and Ellen Craft were far more effective than they ever could have been working apart.

Relationship-building and community-building require both soul-searching and out-reaching. To be able to flourish and not just survive the crisis we will need more trust, more discipline, more willingness to cope and cooperate with one another. No one of us has all the puzzle pieces, no one of us has all the answers. We all need what the other has to offer. Susan L. Taylor, Editor-in-Chief of *Essence* magazine, tells us that

> In every crisis, there is a message. Crises are nature's way of facing change - breaking down old structures, shaking loose negative habits so that something new and better can take their place.[8]

And in order to discern that message, we have to get still enough to hear that voice that can only be heard with the third ear.

References

Chapter 6

1) Natalie Goldberg, *Writing Down the Bones*, (Boston: Shambhala, 1986), p. 40.

2) Dominique Zahan, *Religion, Spirituality and Thought of Traditional Africa*, (Chicago: University of Chicago Press, 1979), p. 10.

3) Toni Grant, *Being a Woman*, (New York: Avon Books, 1988), p.199.

4) John S. Mbiti, *African Religions and Philosophy*, (New York: Anchor Books, Doubleday and Company, Inc.), p. 174.

Chapter 7

1) Louise L. Hay, *Heal Your Body*, (Santa Monica: Hay House, Inc., 1988), p. 34.

2) Jawanza Kunjufu, *Lessons From History: A Celebration in Blackness, Elementary Edition*, (Chicago: African American Images, 1987), p. 43.

3) Earl Ofari Hutchinson, *The Mugging of Black America*, (Chicago: African American Images, 1987), p. 67.

Chapter 8

1) David Hatchett, "...A Conflict of Reasons and

Remedies," *The Crisis*, March 1986, Volume 93, Number 3, p. 39.

2) William Raspberrry, "The Mail on Black Males," *The Washington Post*, August 3, 1989, editorial page.

3) Toni Grant, *Being a Woman*, (New York: Avon Books, 1988), p. 9.

4) Haki Madhubuti, *Black Men: Obsolete, Single, Dangerous? The African Family in Transition*, (Chicago: Third World Press, 1990), p. 12, 160.

5) William Craft, *Running a Thousand Miles to Freedom; or The Escape of William and Ellen Craft from Slavery*, (Miami: Mnemosyne Publishing Co., Inc., 1869), p. 29.

6) Ibid., p. 30.

7) Ibid., p. 50.

8) Susan L. Taylor, quoted by Eric V. Copage in *Black Pearls*, (New York: Quill William Morrow, 1993), p. November 22.

Notes

Notes

Notes